The Birthday Cake

Julie Haydon

It is Mom's birthday.

Where is the birthday cake?

"We will make one," says Dad.

What will we need?

2 eggs

2 tablespoons butter   1 cup sugar   2 cups flour

2/3 cup milk   measuring spoons

Dad turns on the oven to warm it up.

He cracks the eggs into the bowl.

Next I add the butter, sugar, flour, and milk.

The cake mix goes into the tin.

The tin goes into the oven.

Dad and I wash up.

The cake is cooked.

Now it must cool.

Dad puts icing on the cake.

I put candles on the cake.

It is ready.

Mom is home!

Let's surprise her.

Mom likes her presents and cards.

Mom loves her birthday cake.

Now we can eat it!